YOUR FIRST POCKET PET

SUSAN FOX

© **T.F.H. Publications, Inc.**

Distributed in the UNITED STATES to the Pet Trade by T.F.H. Publications, Inc., 1 TFH Plaza, Neptune City, NJ 07753; on the Internet at www.tfh.com; in CANADA by Rolf C. Hagen Inc., 3225 Sartelon St., Montreal, Quebec H4R 1E8; Pet Trade by H & L Pet Supplies Inc., 27 Kingston Crescent, Kitchener, Ontario N2B 2T6; in ENGLAND by T.F.H. Publications, PO Box 74, Havant PO9 5TT; in AUSTRALIA AND THE SOUTH PACIFIC by T.F.H. (Australia), Pty. Ltd., Box 149, Brookvale 2100 N.S.W., Australia; in NEW ZEALAND by Brooklands Aquarium Ltd., 5 McGiven Drive, New Plymouth, RD1 New Zealand; in SOUTH AFRICA by Rolf C. Hagen S.A. (PTY.) LTD., P.O. Box 201199, Durban North 4016, South Africa; in JAPAN by T.F.H. Publications. Published by T.F.H. Publications, Inc.
MANUFACTURED IN THE
UNITED STATES OF AMERICA
BY T.F.H. PUBLICATIONS, INC.

TABLE OF CONTENTS

HOW TO CHOOSE YOUR FIRST POCKET PET

Acquiring your first pet, especially one that is cute and furry, is fun and exciting. When you go into a pet store you will see all kinds of small furry pets. There are so many to choose from! But how do you know which small animal is best for you? What if you bring your new pet home and it isn't what you expected? The best way to avoid disappointment is to know as much as you can about a pet *before* sharing your home with it. Although the pet you want might be cute, you should think about more than its looks. Perhaps the pet you want tends to nip, maybe it is noisy, or maybe it is messy and will be more work than you expected.

Reading this publication can help you decide which type of pocket pet you want, and you will be better prepared to care for it. You will also have a better idea about whether the pet you have wanted is the right one for you and whether you can properly care for it.

Every pet has its fans— people who are fascinated by it for reasons that they might not find easy to explain. Perhaps you want a guinea pig because a neighbor has one, or maybe you really want a hamster so you can build fortlike tubes and tunnels for it to explore.

No matter which type you choose, remember that you want a pet that is friendly and one that you can eventually hold. If a pet store does not have the pet that you want,

Gerbils are very appealing to children and make delightful pets. They are lively and curious and will form a strong bond with their owner with regular handling. Photo by I. Francais.

see whether they can order the pet for you; also, try to visit more than just one pet shop.

Caring for your first pet should be a good experience. If it's not, you might not want another pet for a long time, and then you would miss out on the fun of owning one!

Both children and adults like small furry animals. Chances are good that a child's first pet will be one of the small furry "pocket pets" such as a hamster, mouse, gerbil, rat, rabbit, or one of the other animals discussed in this publication. Although some of these little pets can fit into your pocket (perhaps

grudgingly), others, such as ferrets and rabbits, are larger and don't really qualify as "pocket" pets, but they— especially when they're babies—are still often thought of that way, which is why we'll be discussing them here.

Because of their small size and gentle nature, these creatures can make perfect first pets. Many of these pocket pets are easy for children to hold and play with, and few are intimidating. Their cute looks and interesting habits are captivating. They are fun to cuddle and play with and interesting to watch. It is fun, for example, to see your hamster

3

run on its exercise wheel or happily stuff its cheek pouches with food.

Many kinds of pocket pets can be affectionate and enjoy being played with and cuddled. Soft and furry, pocket pets are comforting and nice to stroke. Almost all types of small animals are nocturnal, which means they are asleep during most of the day. Your pet will be most active and playful at night. At night when you are sleeping, your pet will make many noises. You might hear it gnawing, cracking seeds, drinking water, and playing on its toys. One of the more exciting aspects of small animals is that they are easy to breed, and unlike dogs and cats, their offspring are sometimes easy to find homes for.

As you read, keep the following four questions in mind. First, do you want a pet that is playful and welcomes human interaction? If you want a playful, interactive pet, you might be disappointed with a guinea pig or a hamster. These pets are often content to play by themselves, whereas pets such a rat or a ferret needs to play with its owner in order to thrive. Read the section "The Right Pet For You" to learn what kind of pet each animal makes.

Second, what is the lifespan of the animal you are considering? This is an important consideration, especially with long-lived animals such as ferrets, chinchillas, and rabbits. Ferrits and rabbits can live more than five years, and a chinchilla can live a dozen years. Do you think you will still be interested in caring for such a pet several years from now? If you think that your life will become busier (for example, more after-school activities), then a long-lived animal might be a poor choice. A better selection might be a rat or a gerbil, which will live for only about three years. Before you decide on a pet, consider how long your enthusiasm will last.

Third, how much time do you have to care for a pet? Some animals, such as ferrets, are demanding and require a great deal of attention. Each day a ferret's cage will need to be tidied, and the ferret will need to be let out of its cage to play. Some pets, such as guinea pigs, are messy and will need their cage frequently cleaned, whereas other pets, such as gerbils, are cleaner and can go much longer between cage cleanings. If neglected, some animals might lose their tameness and become skittish. Many pets become bored and unhappy if you never play with them.

It is important to remember that there is no such thing as a no-maintenance pet. Some pets just require less time for their care. Your pet will depend on you for all its needs. Unlike a dog or a cat, which can demand attention, a pocket pet sitting in its cage can easily be ignored. Of the pocket pets, only the guinea pig can whistle for your attention. With the others, only the smell of your neglected pet's home will attract your attention.

Fourth, if the pet will belong to a child, how much help will the child's parents give? Children always promise

Ferrets are full of fun and have loads of personality, but they do require a good deal of attention. They are great for people who like to play a lot. Photo by I. Francais.

to look after a pet, but parents must realize that in many cases the pet's welfare will be partly their responsibility too. Parents cannot expect young children to be solely responsible for their pets; they must help them. A parent's involvement might be as simple as stopping at the pet store to buy food and bedding, but it might involve more primary care, such as helping to feed the pet and to clean its cage. Some young children must be supervised when playing with their pets. Even a tame pet can have sharp nails that could frighten a child.

Depending on age and maturity, a child can help with some of the daily chores and then assume more responsibility as he gets older. Because of their small size, children sometimes have a difficult time cleaning the large cage of some pets, such as rabbits, whereas a gerbil's cage is easier for them to clean without help. Owning a pet is one of the pleasures of childhood. While pet ownership can help in teaching children responsibility, parents must realize that they are the guiding force in this learning experience. Merely owning a pet will not teach a child to be responsible.

Children do not have long attention spans. Once the novelty of owning a pet wears off, caring for it can become one more chore. Continued parental involvement can help children to maintain their own interest. The opportunity to buy new toys for their pets to play with helps some children remain enthusiastic. Children like to save their allowances to buy toys for their pets,

This female golden satin hamster is the vision of health. She's alert and curious and will make a great pet for the right person. Photo by M. Gilroy.

because that allows them to role-play as the care-taker.

CHOOSING A HEALTHY POCKET PET

Even though pocket pets comprise many species of animals ranging in size from a mouse to a rabbit, healthy small pet mammals share common characteristics. Healthy animals have thick, shiny fur and clear, bright eyes. They should look solid and a little plump. When you hold the one you want, it should not feel frail and listless. Do not choose an animal that has runny eyes or a runny nose, a rough or thin coat, lumps, or scabs. Dirty or matted fur near the animal's tail can be a sign of diarrhea.

The pet store where you buy your pet should have clean, uncrowded cages. Animals kept in dirty, crowded cages are less likely to be healthy. Ideally, the pet store should separate cages for the male and female animals; otherwise, a female could become pregnant if not separated soon enough from the males.

A good choice is an animal that is active and curious. Do not choose one that struggles frantically and does not calm down when it is held. An animal's temperament, or personality, does not usually have any bearing on its health. However, keep in mind that a shy or aggressive animal (no matter how attractively colored) will not be as much fun as a naturally friendly one. With the exception of ferrets, which sometimes playbite like puppies when young, the pet you choose should not bite or nip. This is an unusual and undesirable trait for most domesticated pocket pets. An animal that bites once will often bite again.

Because many types of small pocket pets do not live for more than a few years, it is important to choose a young animal so that you can enjoy your pet as long as possible. Young animals are also easier to tame. Although fanciers of the different types of pocket pets might prefer females or males, any differences in tamability and temperament between the sexes are not that great. Both males and females will make good pets. Your pet might be frightened and nervous when you first bring it home, so you should let your pet get used to its new home before you play with it.

HOUSING YOUR PET

Depending on the type of pet you buy, you will need to house it in a wire cage or in a glass or plastic aquarium. A wooden cage is not recommended, as your pet may chew the wood and escape. Also, wooden cages are difficult to keep clean, because they tend to absorb urine and other odors.

Each type of pet has certain requirements regarding the amount of space it needs and the shape of the space. Guinea pigs do not climb cage bars like hamsters and mice. A horizontal cage with lots of floor space is best for them. Other small animals, such as mice, rats, ferrets, and chinchillas, are acrobatic and athletic. They appreciate climbing space in two- and three-story townhouses. Animals that like to dig, such as gerbils, do well in cages that have room for deep bedding, such as a bottom tray with high sides to catch any bedding that spills out.

These chinchillas would not be very happy nor healthy for very long in this small aquarium. Be sure you choose the right size and type of housing for your new pet. Photo by V. Serbin.

Many manufacturers label their cages for specific kinds of small pets, such as hamsters or rabbits. These labels are usually reliable guidelines.

You will notice that I am here recommending cages of certain minimum dimensions for each type of small animal. It is not really practical or necessary to take a tape measure into a pet store to measure the cages. You can generally rely upon the cage labels and a pet store employee's recommendation. But if you have any doubts, take a tape measure along when purchasing your pet's cage.

Do not worry if you do not see a cage labelled for your type of pet. Some species' needs overlap. Hamsters, gerbils, and mice can usually be housed in the same kind of cage, but rats need more room. While cages designed for one type of small animal can often be used to house another (e.g., gerbils in hamster cages, rabbits in guinea pig cages, and chinchillas in ferret cages), you must pay attention to the space between the wire cage bars. For example, the narrow feet of a guinea pig can fall through the large floor spaces of a wire cage suitable for rabbits, which can lead to twisted feet and other injuries. (The section on housing guinea pigs gives more information on buying this pet's home.)

Make sure that you buy the right cage for your pet. If you buy the wrong cage, you could have an unpleasant experience, such as an escaped pet. Pet stores offer a wide variety of attractive homes, from practical wire-mesh cages to

These domestic mice will explore every nook and cranny of this little plastic house. Plastic toys and accessories are good for pocket pets. Ease of cleaning is one major advantage. Photo by M.Gilroy.

colorful, castlelike cages with interconnecting parts. The pet store where you buy your pet should have a cage that appeals to you.

A cage for your pocket pet must be a comfortable home. A basic rule is to buy as large a cage as you can afford. All small animals need enough room for eating, sleeping, and toilet areas. Many types of small pets will establish a bathroom area away from their food and sleep areas, although it should be noted

that some species, such as mice, are not that tidy.

You might be shocked when a cage for a pet costs five times as much as the pet itself. To save money, you might ask for a smaller cage, but that can be a mistake. A cage that is too small will get dirty and smell much sooner. A cage that is too confining also can lead to abnormal behavior and an irritable pet. Remember, your pet will spend most of its life in its cage, which needs, therefore,

Their cage is a safe haven for these guinea pigs. Do not trust dogs or cats around pocket pets until you are sure there won't be any danger to them. Photo by L. Van der Meid.

to be roomy. A cage is a one-time expense that will last for the life of your pet and possibly for the lives of several additional pets.

The word "cage" sounds unpleasant to some people. Some pet owners, especially of larger pets, such as rabbits and ferrets, often feel it is cruel to keep their friends in a cage and best to let them

roam free in the house. However, without supervision a loose pet is a hazard. Your pet can chew electrical cords and possibly start a fire! If it makes you feel better, think of your pet's cage as its bedroom. The cage is your pet's refuge and gives it safety and a sense of security.

It is imperative that you select a cage that is solidly constructed and well designed. Quality cages made of wire share certain features. There should be no sharp edges, either inside or out. For larger pets such as rabbits and ferrets, welded seams rather than clipped corners are often sturdier and more durable. A strong door latch will help prevent pets from escaping. The door should fasten securely so that it cannot be pushed or pulled at the corners. In addition, the door should be large enough for you to easily reach your hand into the animal's cage. The cage should be designed so that cleaning and maintenance are easy. The cage tray should slide out or the top of the cage should separate easily from the base. Ideally, a finish should be applied that makes the cage tray better

Wood shavings make a perfect bed for these pygmy hedgehogs. Photo by I. Francais.

able to resist rust and corrosion.

CAGE PLACEMENT

Place the cage in an area where you can enjoy your new pet. Your pet should be part of your family, not banished from it. While certain types of small pets, such as rabbits and guinea pigs, can be kept outdoors in parts of the country where the temperatures are suitable, most pocket pets should be kept inside your house. Because of car exhaust fumes, pesticides, fertilizers, and poor temperature control, the garage is an unhealthy location for your pet. Pets kept outside are more likely to be forgotten and neglected compared to those that are kept inside.

Avoid exposing your pet to rapidly changing temperatures. Do not place the cage near a heating or air conditioning vent. Nor should you place your pet's cage near a window. Windows can be drafty and can expose your

Beddings treated with chlorophyll will help reduce odors, especially with larger pets like rabbits, ferrets, and chinchillas. Photo by L. Van der Meid.

HOW TO CHOOSE YOUR FIRST POCKET PET

The cage sizes and types presented in this book are comfortable for the various pocket pets. They are not the *only* options, however. These guinea pigs are being kept in a specially designed glass-walled enclosure that is a major part of the room décor. Photo by P. Gurney.

pet to hours of hot sunlight, which could be fatal.

Most pets can tolerate a house or apartment's normal variations in temperature, light, and humidity, but some species are less hardy than others. For example, chinchillas are susceptible to overheating and ferrets are sensitive to chills and drafts.

Make your pet's home a pleasant part of a room. Set the cage on a dresser, desk, or table. It is best not to place your pet's cage on the floor. Other pets, such as dogs and cats, can terrify your new pet by sniffing and staring at it. Even without good vision, most pocket pets are sensitive to sudden movements. They can be frightened and stressed by people walking around and near their cage. In addition, the temperature near the floor is often cooler than on a desk or dresser. If you must place your pet's cage on the floor, tuck the

A chocolate mouse peeks out of her pal's pocket.

Whatever type of house you choose for your pocket pet, make sure the animal cannot escape. These small creatures are notorious for their Houdini-like abilities. Photo by M. Gilroy

pleasant smelling. Pine, aspen, and pine shavings treated with chlorophyll work well as bedding. Many small animal organizations now recommend that shavings of the red cedar tree, which are reddish in color and fragrant smelling, not be used, because evidence suggests that they can cause respiratory problems in some small animals.

Many sophisticated products made from recycled paper are available as bedding for small animals. Many of these products are designed to control or eliminate odor, thus promoting a healthier home for your pet. They cost more but are worth it, because they let you go longer between cleaning your pet's cage. You might be tempted to

cage into a corner so that your pet will detect movements on only two sides of its home. If you think your pet might get cold, give it extra nesting material.

Most small pets are enthusiastic chewers. Be sure to keep items such as clothing and books away from your pet's cage. If your pet can pull such items into its cage to chew, it will.

BEDDING

All small mammals need bedding in their cage. Bedding keeps your pet warm, dry, and clean by absorbing moisture. It provides a place for your pet to sleep and can help reduce odor. Some types of bedding allow your pet to engage in its natural behaviors, such as burrowing.

Wood shavings are one of the most popular types of small animal beddings. Shavings are inexpensive and

This female agouti mouse feels quite cozy and secure in her tennis ball "nest." Photo by M. Gilroy.

use newspaper. Although the ink is non-toxic, it will rub off and make your pet dirty.

Many small animals like to play in and burrow through hay, which you can place on top of their regular bedding. Some animals, such as hamsters, rats, mice, and gerbils, need nesting material, which they shred and make into a sleeping nest. Pet stores sell nesting material, or you can use paper towels, unscented tissue paper, or an old sock. Be careful of giving your pet material such as cotton wool. Long fibers can sometimes wrap around a pet's toe and might cause the loss of the toe if the problem caused by the fibers is not caught in time.

ACCESSORIES

Always place your pet's food in a dish. Heavy ceramic dishes that your pet cannot turn over or metal dishes that clip to the side of the cage are best.

Provide fresh water in a gravity-demand water bottle. These bottles are sold in pet stores. Place the bottle away from your pet's sleeping area in case it leaks. Do not use an open dish to provide your pet with water. Most pets make the water dirty by filling the dish with bedding and food. Larger pets might even spill the dish, making their cage wet.

Small animals prefer to sleep in a hiding place with walls. This gives them a sense of security that nothing can sneak up behind them. Most small animals are nocturnal and appreciate being able to retreat into the security of a cozy "bedroom." Provide your pet with a nest box in which to sleep. Your pet will also

Newspaper bedding will make your pocket pet's fur dirty and grimy. Don't use it. Photo by I. Francais.

Some homemade accessories work just fine for pocket pets. Mice, particularly, will get great fun out of a paper towel roll. Photo by G. Axelrod.

This is a young male Siamese rat enjoying a new toy. Photo by M. Gilroy.

Exercise wheels are ideal for mice, rats, gerbils, and other small, active pocket pets. Photo by Isabelle Francais.

hide in its nest box when it wants privacy. Pet stores sell ceramic, plastic, wood, and cardboard nest boxes for small furry pets. Ceramic homes cannot be chewed, but they might be accidentally broken. The wood and cardboard types are designed to be gnawed and chewed by your pet. For smaller pocket pets, you can make a nest box from an empty milk or oatmeal carton.

TOYS

Your pet needs some type of entertainment or it will become bored and listless. Your pet will be more active and interesting to watch if you provide it with toys. Exercise wheels, hammocks, rope swings, chew toys, and ladders are some of the toys that your pet might enjoy.

Expect your pet to also gnaw and chew on its toys. The teeth of rodents and rabbits are constantly growing. Those animals need to gnaw on hard wood blocks and other objects to keep their teeth in good condition.

Most small animals will enjoy playing with almost anything you put into their cages. Toys can be used interchangeably by different species. Many small animals, including rats, gerbils, mice, and hamsters, like to explore and are fascinated with hiding places. Toys made for ferrets, such as tunnel logs and nest balls, can be used by all of these small pets. Animals that like to climb, such as rats and mice, can use wooden ladders and natural wood perches made for parrots. Rabbits and guinea pigs can be given

Black and cream hooded rats amuse themselves on bird toys. Expect pocket pets to gnaw on wooden toys. Photo by M. Gilroy.

A 4-week-old agouti gerbil "hanging out" in a wooden toy. Photo by M. Gilroy.

This is a female dominant spot hamster peering out of her little house. Photo by M. Gilroy.

Ferrets are extremely playful. These balls on springs will keep a ferret happy for hours on end. Photo by Isabelle Francais.

Hamsters enjoy playing "peek-a-boo" in hollow toys. Photo by M. Gilroy.

This African pygmy hedgehog will probably curl up inside the log for a nap. Photo by I. Francais.

alfalfa blocks, hanging parrot wood blocks for chewing, and small balls with bells to push around. Most wooden toys made for parakeets and parrots are safe to use for small rodents.

Do not overcrowd your pet's cage with too many toys. Your pet could accidentally get hurt (for example, a toy could fall and trap it), and a crowded cage leaves too little room. You should rotate your pet's toys. This will help prevent your pet from growing tired of playing with the same ones. The toys will also need to be washed and cleaned. Finally, do not forget that most small animals, ferrets, rabbits, and rats in particular, thrive on human attention. Play with them so they will be attached to you.

It is fun to take your pet out of its cage to play. You can let your pet explore and play in the room where you keep its cage. Before doing this, you must "pet-proof" the room. Small mammals are natural gnawers, burrowers, and escape-artists. Furnace grills, appliance grills, and air conditioning vents should be blocked off so that your pet cannot escape.

Never let your pet loose in the room without supervising him. (It is safest to keep the door closed to the room in which your pet is playing.) Pets can chew electrical cords, books, and papers; rabbits can scratch the carpet in the corner of a room; ferrets and rats might dig up and eat houseplants. Hamsters enjoy exercise balls, which allow them to safely cruise around the home on smooth-surface floors. Harnesses and leashes

Never let your small pet loose in the room without careful supervision. Ferrets, in particular, are notorious escape artists and can squeeze themselves into the tiniest of crevices. Photo by I. Francais.

A playpen cage can be used inside or out to keep your pocket pet safe and contained. Here, the children are enjoying their guinea pigs in the yard. Photo by L. Van der Meid.

Untippable dishes are a real asset. Most pocket pets think nothing of sleeping in their food dishes, so at least if the food doesn't spill there's a better chance the cage will stay tidy. Photo by M. Gilroy.

can be used to help supervise exploring by ferrets and rabbits.

An alternative to letting your pet loose in a room is a pet containment system sold at pet stores. A wall of plastic is designed to unroll and fasten together, providing your pet with a safe playpen. This flexible playpen can allow you to play with your pet in almost any room of your home without having to worry about your pet's escaping.

Whenever and wherever your pet is playing outside its cage, it might leave droppings. Some pets such as rabbits and ferrets can be housebroken. Place some of your pet's dirty bedding in a small animal litter pan. Let your pet loose to play in the "proofed" room containing the litter box. Place the litter box against the wall so that your pet is most likely to encounter it.

CLEANING

There is no escape from having to clean your pet's home. Manufacturers have developed products that make it easier and that let you go longer between cleanings, but at some point the cleaning job must be done.

Bedding materials that control the development of ammonia and pan liners, which allow you to completely remove the bedding from your pet's home without spilling any of it, are two time-saving products.

The homes of most small pets should be thoroughly cleaned at least once a week, although some, such as gerbils, can go a bit longer between cleanings. If the cage smells even after dumping out the bedding, use a wash cloth and warm soapy water to wash the cage. Then completely rinse and dry the cage. Your pet will chew and soil its nest box, which should be replaced as needed. Many small animals use a corner of their cage for a bathroom. The bedding in this area can be replaced every day or so to prevent odor.

You will notice that your pet spends hours washing and brushing its fur with its tongue and paws. While you can depend on your pocket pet to keep itself naturally clean, your pet will depend on you to keep its cage clean. If its cage is not clean, your pet will have a harder time keeping itself clean. The more animals kept in a cage, the more often you will have to clean it. The smell of a pet's cage is one of the most common complaints of small animal owners. Your pet's cage will smell only if you do not clean it often enough. The stinky ammonia odor that develops in your pet's cage is unpleasant to you and unhealthy for your pet. Ammonia is a severe irritant and very bad for the health of your pet. In between cleaning your pet's cage, use bedding with odor-masking agents, such as chlorophyll shavings, or use odor-control bedding made from recycled paper. Remember, if your pet's home smells, it is because it is dirty; clean it and the odor will go away.

FEEDING

The importance of feeding a good diet cannot be overestimated. The quality of your pet's diet can affect its health, appearance, ability to reproduce, lifespan, and even

Some commercially available foods include both staple nutrient ingredients and special treats, thereby managing to combine good nutrition with tempting delicacies. Photo courtesy of Sun Seed Company, Inc.

Sturdy dishwasher-safe food and water bowls that are easy to install and remove make the task of regular cleaning much easier, helping to guarantee that necessary good hygienic standards are maintained in feeding and watering your pets. Photo courtesy of Lixit Animal Care Products.

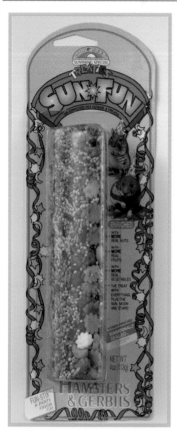

Vitamin-enriched foods that contain tidbits specially formulated to appeal to gerbils make it easy to provide your pets with good nutrition and a little bit of party atmosphere at the same time. Photo courtesy of Sun Seed Company, Inc.

Guinea pigs enjoy healthy treats like carrots and lettuce. Photo by I. Francais.

its temperament. Because pocket pets have been used as laboratory animals and kept as pets for so long, their dietary needs are fairly well known. It is simple to provide your pet with good nutrition. Pet stores sell packaged foods for all the pets discussed in this publication. Most small furry animals like to nibble on food throughout the day and night, so be sure your pet always has food in its dish.

Small pets enjoy food treats. Fresh fruits and vegetables found in your kitchen make good treats for your pet. Whatever moist foods you feed your pet can spoil and make your pet sick. Remove any uneaten moist food after ten minutes or feed your pet only as much as it can eat in one sitting.

Pet food manufacturers make many types of healthy treats for all kinds of small pets. You can give your pet treats to win its trust, to train it, or just because you enjoy watching your pet eat a tasty snack. Hard treat foods and chew sticks also help your pet keep its constantly growing teeth trim.

Rawhide Oodles are great for hamsters, rats, guinea pigs, gerbils, and mice. Gnawing on Oodles helps these small animals keep their teeth the proper length, a necessary consideration for animals with ongoing tooth growth.

HOW TO CHOOSE YOUR FIRST POCKET PET

POCKET PET AILMENTS

For the most part, pocket pets are a very hardy group, which is one of the reasons why they are so popular.

Your pet will not usually show symptoms of illness until late in the course of a disease. Like other pets such as birds, the ability to hide an illness is believed to be self-protective behavior. In the wild, an animal that acts sick is easy prey for predators. By the time you realize your pet is sick, it has probably been sick for quite some time. In many cases, treatment is difficult, because the condition is so advanced at the time of detection.

Sick small animals usually show similar types of symptoms. Obvious signs of illness include discharge from the eyes or nose. Once you have cared for your pet for a while, you will know its normal behavior, for example, how much it eats and when it is most active. Any changes in your pet's normal behavior, such as lethargy and reduced appetite, could mean it is sick. If your pet shows any other symptoms of illness, such as weight loss and a rough coat, you should consult a veterinarian immediately. The longer you wait the sicker your pet could become.

Bacteria and viruses can cause infectious diseases. Good husbandry, such as keeping the cage clean, can usually prevent such diseases.

Right: Be sure to check the skin. Fleas are not common on pocket pets, but any skin rash is suspicious. Photo by I. Francais.

If you have any doubts at all about the health of your pet, visit a vet! Vets care for all animals, great and small. Photo by V. Serbin.

Be sure to examine your new pet for physical abnormalities. The bump on this rabbit's neck *is* normal for this animal, but similar swellings on another kind of animal might be an indication of illness. Photo by Isabelle Francais.

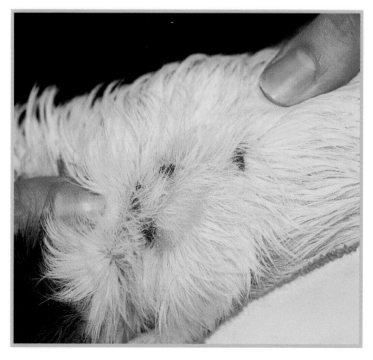

CHINCHILLAS

Chinchillas are rodents that look like plump squirrels with large, round ears and a short, furry tail. Their kangaroolike hind legs help them to hop and jump quickly, and they use their small front hands to hold food. Chinchillas originally came from high elevations in the Andes Mountains of South America. These plant-eating rodents were brought to the United States in the 1920s. Chinchillas were bred on fur farms for their soft, dense, silky coats, which are among the finest in the world. Instead of a single hair, seventy to eighty fine hairs grow from each hair root.

Domestic chinchillas are different from their wild relatives. In the wild, chinchillas can leap up to eight feet high in the air to escape a predator, but chinchillas of domesticated strains can leap less than three feet.

WHICH KIND?

Originally chinchillas came in only a pretty gray color. Although gray is still the most common color, over the years of their domestication chinchillas have been bred in many other colors. Beige, black, and white chinchillas are also sometimes offered for sale.

Unlike the situation with many other small furry pets, the female chinchilla is larger than the male. Chinchillas are full grown when they are about six months old. Adults weigh between one and one and one-half pounds and

A baby chinchilla in a tissue box. Photo by M. Gilroy.

measure ten to fifteen inches long.

MORE THAN ONE?

You can keep a single chinchilla as long as you give it plenty of attention. If you want more than one chinchilla, you should buy them at the same time. Two females or two males can be housed together as long as you get them both when they are young. If you have a male and a female, they will have babies. Do not keep more than two chinchillas in one cage or they might fight.

THE RIGHT PET FOR YOU?

Chinchillas have a friendly disposition and can become very tame. They are gentle and curious but timid with new people and situations.

It takes time and patience to tame a chinchilla. Even

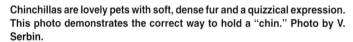

Chinchillas are lovely pets with soft, dense fur and a quizzical expression. This photo demonstrates the correct way to hold a "chin." Photo by V. Serbin.

CHINCHILLAS

Right: An adult male chinchilla. Because of their heavy coats chinchillas prefer cooler temperatures. Photo by M. Gilroy.

Below: Handle your young chinchilla frequently so that it will be tame and friendly when it grows up. Photo by I. Francais.

The chinchilla's teeth are properly orange to yellow. Be sure to provide rawhide products to help them keep their teeth the proper length. Photo by M. Gilroy.

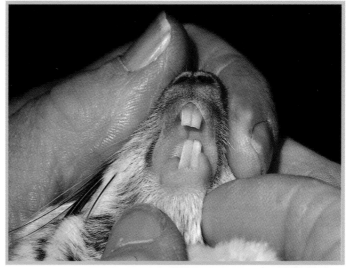

Chinchillas need regular dust baths to keep their fur clean. They seem to enjoy them immensely! Photo by V. Serbin.

tame chinchillas will still be startled by sudden movements and loud noises. Like other small animal pets such as rabbits, chinchillas that are neglected will not stay friendly. Tame chinchillas are usually docile and will not struggle. If handled improperly, chinchillas can become frightened and lose tufts of their hair. Chinchillas need to be handled so that they remain friendly.

Your pet needs to play outside its cage each day. Chinchillas are voracious chewers and might gnaw books and other items. You need to watch your chinchilla while it exercises.

Because of their soft fur and large appealing eyes, many people want to cuddle and pet chinchillas. However, chinchillas do not like to be picked up and held that much. They are energetic and like to bound around a room. You can coax your pet into pausing and visiting during

its exploration if you offer a treat.

Chinchillas are nocturnal and are usually asleep during the day. Although they are most active at night, chinchillas can adapt to late afternoon playtimes. Chinchillas are a long-term commitment because they live a long time, between ten and fifteen years. Because of their long lifespan, chinchillas are good pets for adults. Children might not stay interested in a chinchilla for that long.

Use one hand to hold the chinchilla near the base of its tail and use your other hand to cradle the chinchilla's body against your own. Chinchillas are usually docile and will not struggle. Chinchillas have the softest fur of all small animal pets. When you hold a chinchilla you will be amazed at the incredible softness of its coat.

Your pet's beautiful fur requires special care. Chinchillas need a daily dust bath

to remove dirt, loose hair, and oil from their fur. The oil comes from their skin and from your hands. If you do not give your pet a dust bath, its coat can become dull and matted looking. The "dust" in which it bathes is usually volcanic ash, which you can buy at your local pet store. Use a container deep enough to hold at least two inches of dust and large enough so that your chinchilla can somersault and flip around in the dust. A glass or hard plastic container with sides about five inches high is ideal. Place the dust bowl in the cage for a short time each day. Change the dust every day. It is very entertaining to watch your chinchilla take a dust bath.

SELECTING YOUR CHINCHILLA

Chinchillas are weaned at six to eight weeks. Some young chinchillas are stressed from weaning, and many breeders recommend buying a chinchilla when it is three to four months old. Like most other animals, young chinchillas are easier to tame than older ones. Chinchillas between two and three months old are cute, curious, and easy to tame. Young chinchillas' teeth are white and gradually turn dark orange with age. Have the pet store employee show you the chinchilla's teeth so that you know whether or not you are buying an older chinchilla.

Because of their higher price, individual chinchillas might sometimes remain in a pet store for quite a while before being sold. As long as the store employees are handling the chinchilla, it should be relatively tame, friendly, and socialized to

A clean cage with food, water, and a nice bed make for a very happy chinchilla. Photo by V. Serbin

people. However, if the chinchilla is older and skittish, consider waiting for a friendlier individual.

HOUSING AND ACCESSORIES

Large cages give active chinchillas room to play. Chinchillas do well when housed in two- and three-story wire-frame ferret cages. While chinchillas are good apartment pets, the large cages they require take up more space than many other small pets' cages. Your pet will appreciate a cage with a ramp leading up to a perching platform. The cage can include ramps, a large exercise wheel, and branches. Also provide a wooden sleeping box for your chinchilla.

One adult chinchilla should be kept in a two foot square cage. A pair of chinchillas should be housed in a cage measuring 40 inches long by 24 inches wide by 24 inches high. Breeders do not agree on whether chinchillas should be kept on a solid or a wire floor. To prevent their fur from becoming dirty, some breeders recommend not housing chinchillas directly on top of their bedding, while others state that housing them directly on wire tends to stress them. As long as you clean your pet's cage often enough (every seven to ten days), both the cage and your chinchilla should stay clean. Use a layer of pine shavings on the cage floor.

Chinchillas are very clean animals and don't have a noticeable odor. They do not drink much water and consequently produce little urine. Most chinchillas

While every encounter with your chinchilla need not involve food, treats are useful in taming your pet. Photo by V. Serbin.

deposit their droppings in one area of their cage, so their cages are easy to clean.

Chinchillas are sensitive to changes in temperature. Their dense fur keeps them warm, and they can become stressed when too hot. When chinchillas are stressed, their coats quickly lose their healthy condition and become matted. Do your best to keep your pet's home at a constant—and not too warm—temperature.

FEEDING

Feed your pet a diet specifically formulated for chinchillas. If this food is unavailable, you can feed

your chinchilla rabbit pellets.

In addition to the pellets, give a handful of hay or a block of cubed hay each day for necessary roughage. Your chinchilla will enjoy treats such as raisins, sunflower seeds, and small pieces of apple, carrot, or celery. Chinchillas are sensitive to stomach upset or diarrhea from feeding too many treats. Be careful to offer only a small amount of these treats, such as no more than one raisin a day.

Chinchillas also need wood chews to help keep their teeth trim and in good condition. Provide fresh drinking water in a water bottle.

FERRETS

Ferrets are quiet, clean, and forever playful. They are related to the otter, weasel, mink, marten, ermine, badger, and skunk. Photo by M. Gilroy.

While at a friend's house you might have been startled by the appearance of a long, slinky ferret. The ferret jumped toward you, then dashed away. Bounding about the room, twisting and leaping in the air, the ferret hissed and chortled as it invited you to play.

The playful ferret is the domesticated descendant of the European polecat. Ferrets have been raised in Europe since Roman times. They were imported into the United States in the 1870s. Ferrets were used as hunting animals, trained to go into holes to drive out pests such as rabbits and rats. If properly introduced, ferrets can often get along well with other pets, such as dogs and cats, but not with other small animals such as hamsters, rabbits, and guinea pigs.

The domestic ferret belongs to the family Mustelidae, the same scientific family as skunks. Members of this family are known for the strong, unpleasant odor they can discharge from scent glands located near their anus.

WHICH KIND?

Albino and sable are the two basic ferret colors. Sable ferrets come in different shades of black, brown, gray, and chestnut. The feet and tail of both the albino and sable are of a darker color than the body.

Ferrets are fully grown when they are about six months old. Females usually weigh between one and two pounds and are between twelve to fifteen inches in length. Males are usually larger than females. They weigh between two to three pounds and are about twenty inches in length. Female ferrets are called jills and male ferrets are called hobs.

MORE THAN ONE?

Ferrets can be kept alone, but they do like company. If you start off with one ferret, you can always get it a friend at a later time. As long as you gradually introduce the new ferret to your first ferret, there should be few problems. However, you will probably need another cage for your second ferret. Usually one ferret will be dominant over the other.

THE RIGHT PET FOR YOU?

Ferrets are affectionate, playful, and curious. They

become very tame if bought young and handled often. Ferrets are nocturnal, but they can learn to switch to a daytime schedule. However, carefully consider whether a ferret is the right pet for you. While ferrets are one of most interesting "pocket" pets, they are also the most demanding. Because ferrets live between five and seven years, they are a long-term commitment.

A ferret is like a rambunctious puppy. Like a puppy, a ferret is inquisitive, adventurous, and intelligent. And just as a puppy needs a daily walk, a ferret needs playtime outside its cage each day. This type of commitment is much greater than that required by a guinea pig or hamster.

You must watch your ferret when it is playing outside its cage. Ferrets like to put things into their mouths. Your pet might swallow something, such as a piece of foam from your couch, that could cause an intestinal blockage that could lead to death. That's one reason why the rooms in which a ferret explores must be "ferret-proofed"—made safe for the ferret.

While your ferret is young, play with it often to help bond with it. Doing so will make your pet more docile and affectionate. Just like a puppy, a young ferret might nip. You must teach your ferret that biting is unacceptable by saying once, in a firm tone, "No!" and tapping him on the nose with your index finger.

While ferrets make good pets, ferret ownership requires being responsible.

A harness and leash is a must for ferret owners. If there is a downside to owning a ferret, it is that their curiosity could lead to them getting lost. Photo by I. Francais.

Toys make for great ferret fun but avoid soft rubber toys that can be shredded with your ferret's sharp teeth. Photo by I. Francais.

Ferrets love hammock-style beds. Photo by I. Francais.

Ferrets have sharp teeth that need to be cleaned occasionally. Hard foods, like Rawhide Oodles, will help keep your ferret's teeth in good shape. Photo by M. Gilroy.

Many organizations devoted to ferrets do not recommend ferrets for families with children younger than five. When ferrets are playing outside their cage, they have the opportunity to interact with all family members, including very young children. Young children do not know their own strength and do not know how to hold animals. They can accidentally hurt a ferret, and the ferret could respond by biting. Young children should never be allowed to handle your pet without adult supervision. Even though your ferret is tame and friendly, never leave a baby or a small child alone with a ferret. A ferret has sharp teeth and a strong grip. Whereas most small animals belong to single family member, ferrets are more like cats and dogs in that they are considered to be the entire family's pet.

Ferrets wash and groom themselves every day, but they still have a natural musky odor because of their skin and scent glands. This odor is stronger in a ferret that has not been neutered. However, most ferrets that are sold in pet stores are both neutered and descented. Even so, a pet ferret will still smell, because its skin scent glands cannot be removed.

A weekly bath with ferret shampoo will control a ferret's scent and help keep it clean. You will also need to trim your ferret's claws about once a month. The area around your pet's cage will always have a slightly musky odor.

Buying a neutered ferret is always preferable to one

FERRETS

Delightful imps! Photo by I. Francais.

that is unneutered. Besides reduced odor, neutered ferrets are calmer and cannot breed. If you buy a female ferret, it is especially important to buy a neutered animal, since a female that has not been spayed can develop an irreversible and fatal condition if she is not mated when in heat.

Ferrets need annual visits to a veterinarian. They need to be vaccinated against canine distemper and rabies, and annual booster shots are necessary to provide continuous protection.

It is legal to keep ferrets almost every state, but some cities and counties have regulations governing the ownership of pet ferrets. Generally, if ferrets are sold

This is the correct way to hold a ferret, supporting both the front and the back of the body. Photo by M. Gilroy.

Ferrets must have regular baths. Be sure to dry your ferret thoroughly so it doesn't catch a chill after its bath. Photo by I. Francais.

in the pet stores where you live, they are legal to own.

SELECTING

Choose a healthy, friendly ferret, preferably one that is curious and gentle. Expect young ferrets to playbite, but do not choose one that nips and hangs on without letting go. If the ferret you want is not already descented and neutered, you will have to pay to have a veterinarian perform this procedure.

HOUSING AND ACCESSORIES

Ferret cages are available in many styles and sizes.

The cages, which are made of wire mesh, come in single, double, and triple stories. No matter what style, ferrets need a spacious cage. One to two ferrets can be kept in a cage measuring 36 inches long by 18 inches wide by 18 inches high. Ferrets are active animals, and their cage should be large enough for separate sleeping, feeding, and litter box areas.

Ferrets also need sturdy cages. A bored ferret spends much of its time looking for weak spots in its cage. If it can escape, it will. The cage door must always close completely and securely. If a ferret can squeeze part of its head out of the cage door, but cannot fit the rest of its body through, or cannot pull its head back in, it is possible the ferret could accidentally die. If necessary, fasten the cage door with a clip.

Treats will help build trust between you and your new ferret. Photo by I. Francais.

FERRETS

Ferrets like to be a part of their family's activities, so a good location for their cage is often the family or living room. Be sure to keep your pet's cage out of drafts, because ferrets are susceptible to colds and respiratory illnesses.

Most ferret experts recommend that you place pine shavings in the cage tray below the wire screen. Ferrets kept on shavings sometimes eat them and become constipated. Ferrets are clean animals and should be trained to use a litter pan, which will make cage cleaning easier.

Pelleted litter made from recycled paper or plant fiber should be used in the litter pan, not clay. Use a litter scooper to remove the droppings each day. You must keep the pan clean or else your ferret might stop using it. Give your pet a small ferret bed or a hammock in which to sleep. Wash your ferret's bed once a week.

Yes, ferrets can be trained to use the litter box. Consistency is a part of the training process. Be sure the box is always clean and always in the same corner. Photo by I. Francais.

Ferrets can be kept by themselves, in pairs, or even in groups provided they are given a chance to get to know each other first. Photo by M. Gilroy.

FEEDING

Ferrets are carnivorous and need a diet that is high in animal protein and fat. The best food to feed is a commercial ferret diet sold in pet stores. A high-quality dry cat food, such as the type sold only in pet stores, can be fed if ferret food is unavailable. Ferrets have a fast metabolism and eat small meals throughout the day. You pet should always have food in its dish. Small amounts of treats such as fresh fruits and vegetables will be relished by your pet. Provide fresh water in a water bottle.

GERBILS

The gerbil originally came from the deserts and plains of Mongolia and nearby areas, which is why it is sometimes called the Mongolian gerbil. In this rodent's natural habitat, the summers are very hot and the winters are very cold. Gerbils are able to survive in the harsh desert because they live underground in tunnels where the temperature does not fluctuate as much. Gerbils forage at night and are able to derive water metabolically from the foods they eat. Gerbils were first captured for use as laboratory animals, but because they are gentle and easy to care for, they eventually were offered as pets.

Like kangaroos, gerbils have big, strong hind legs that let them quickly hop and leap. In the wild, gerbils use their hind feet to drum on the ground and warn each other of approaching danger. They use their little front feet to hold food and to dig. Like some other nocturnal animals, gerbils have large eyes.

WHICH KIND?

Gerbils come in a variety of colors, including agouti, albino, black, gray, and pied. Their eye color is either black

Opposite page: This is a male agouti gerbil. Agouti is the wild coloring of the Mongolian gerbil. There are black hairs in the golden-brown fur of its back and the underside is white. The tail is covered with fur and there is a tuft at the tip. Photo by M. Gilroy.

This light silver male and black female gerbil will enjoy this toy, which appeals to their burrowing instincts. Photo by M. Gilroy.

These are 4-week-old gerbils. They grow fast on a nutritious gerbil diet of seeds, nuts, and some fresh and dried fruit and vegetables. Photo by M. Gilroy.

Gerbils will come to trust you in time. Hold your hand flat with a treat in the palm and slowly approach your gerbil. In time, it allows you to hold it on your flat hand. Photo by M. Gilroy.

The tip of the gerbil's tail is very delicate and easily broken off. If you must hold a gerbil's tail, do so close to the animal's body. Photo by H. Mayer

or red. Mutations in coat length and texture have not appeared, although they might be developed in the future. Other species of gerbil, such as the Egyptian gerbil, are occasionally offered for sale. This species is smaller than the Mongolian gerbil and also makes a good pet.

Gerbils measure about nine inches in length, including their long, fur-covered tail. Their tails act as props when they sit up and help them leap and turn in the air. Male gerbils are larger than females.

MORE THAN ONE?

Gerbils should be kept in pairs. A gerbil kept by itself will be unhappy. Buy two young gerbils at the same time so they can grow up together. Two females will get along best. Males tend to fight when they get older. A male and a female will have babies. Your gerbils will form a lifelong

bond. You will see your pets groom each other, play-fight, and keep each other warm by sleeping together.

THE RIGHT PET FOR YOU?

Compared to most small pocket pets, gerbils live a long time, between three and five years. Gerbils are easy to care for and cute. Although they are lively and active, they are gentle pets. Compared to other pocket pets, gerbils' most notable characteristic is that they are brave and curious. Because gerbils are friendly and inquisitive, your new pets will sniff your hand when you place it into their cage and might boldly step onto your hand. Gerbils are like adventurers: they do not run from the unknown; they advance and investigate. When your pet wants to find out more about its surroundings, it will stand up on its hind legs and sniff the air.

Make friends with your gerbils by letting them sniff and crawl on your hand. If you offer a food treat on the palm of your hand, you might win their trust sooner. Gerbils make good first pets because they rarely, if ever, bite. If a gerbil is scared, it might first stamp its hind leg as a warning that it might bite. If your pet ever does this, figure out what you did that threatened your pet. The warning behavior of other small pets is more subtle. Gerbils communicate with each other by squeaking and by thumping their back legs.

Gerbils are active at night and during the day. In between periods of activity, they take long naps. Gerbils are fun to watch. Their favorite entertainment is digging and

This male black gerbil has filled his pouches with food and is now having a little drink. Photo by M. Gilroy.

burrowing through the bedding in their cage. Gerbils kick their bedding into huge piles against one side of their cage, then rebuild the pile against the other side.

Your pets should have toys inside their cage with which

to play. You can buy a solid-frame exercise wheel at a pet store. (Do not use a wire mesh exercise wheel, because your pet's tail could get caught in the wire.) Gerbils like running on an exercise wheel, although they are not as pas-

An exercise wheel is great for gerbils and keeps them happy for hours. It also helps them keep their weight at a healthy level, especially if you are inclined to give them too many high-calorie treats. Photo by I. Francais.

Gerbils are nocturnal creatures. It is best to keep them in some room other than your bedroom. The rustlings will surely keep you awake as the gerbil scurries around on its nightly rounds. Photo by M. Gilroy.

sionate about running on a wheel as hamsters. Your pets will happily spend time sleeping and darting in and out of plastic tubes and tunnels designed for small animals. You can make your own toys for your pets, such as cardboard tubes and fruit tree branches.

Gerbils should be allowed to play outside their cage. They are curious and like to explore their surroundings. Watch them closely. Gerbils can run fast and may be difficult to catch. Never grab your pets by their tail, especially by the tuft of fur at the tip of their tails. Your gerbil can lose the skin and fur on its tail, and the tuft will not grow back. Most gerbils are fairly bold and will not hide or run away when they are playing outside their cage. You can get your pets to return to their cage by offering a treat.

Gerbils do not mind being held. Some gerbils will climb onto your hand, and you can then pick them up. Otherwise, pick up your pet by scooping your hand underneath your gerbil's belly. Your pet will hold still for a few moments, but it might soon want to be let down to play. For added security, hold the base of your pet's tail, but not the tip. If your gerbil struggles to get away, return it to the cage so that you do not accidentally drop or hurt your pet.

Gerbils have almost no odor. Because they came from the dry desert, gerbils do not drink much water, and they produce only a small amount of urine and tiny hard droppings. Your pet's cage will not need to be cleaned as often as the cages of most other types of small pets. Unless the cage begins to smell, your gerbils' home can be cleaned every ten to fourteen days.

It is not legal to keep gerbils as pets in California. The California Department of Fish and Game has banned gerbils because of concerns that if gerbils become established in the wild, they could damage crops and displace native wildlife.

CHOOSING YOUR GERBILS

Buy your gerbils when

Argente male gerbil. Photo by M. Gilroy.

The gerbil you choose should have a lively and inquisitive nature. Its eyes should be bright and clear. Its coat should be glossy and smooth with no sores or lumps. Photo by I. Francais.

they are between four and eight weeks of age or about two to three inches in body length. Select gerbils that are bold and inquisitive. A gerbil that climbs onto your hand will make a good pet.

HOUSING AND ACCESSORIES

Because gerbils spend a lot of time digging and kicking shavings and food out of their cage, an aquarium is often the best housing choice.

A pair of gerbils can be kept in a ten-gallon or twenty-gallon aquarium with a secure wire-screen cover. An aquarium will keep the area around your pet's cage from becoming messy. Of course wire cages make good

Female gerbils get along very well together but two males may fight. Photo by H. Mayer.

Even young toddlers can enjoy pet gerbils. Just be sure an adult supervises playtime between gerbils and young children. Photo by I. Francais.

Gerbils are cute but smart and tricky too! If they are frightened they will lie down and play dead until the danger has passed. Photo by M. Gilroy.

One grape constitutes a large meal for a small gerbil. Photo by H. Mayer.

homes too, but they allow bedding to fall out. To prevent the area around their pets' homes from becoming untidy, some gerbil owners keep their pets' wire cages inside a cat litter pan to catch any bedding that spills out.

Provide a deep layer of bedding, about four inches, inside your pets' cage so they can dig and burrow. Provide your gerbils with a nest box in which to sleep. You can buy a nest box at a pet store or make one from an old cereal box. Toys designed for gerbils, hamsters, and mice can be placed inside your pets' cage. Your pets will be more entertaining to watch if they have toys in their cage on which to play.

FEEDING

Feed your herbivorous pets a commercial diet made for gerbils. The mix typically includes seeds, grains, and nuts. Give daily treats of well-washed small pieces of vegetable and fruit. Do not feed too much at one time, since doing so will give gerbils diarrhea. A handful of cubed or loose hay will provide needed fiber. Gerbils like treats that you can buy at pet stores. Dog biscuits are favorite snacks. Some individuals like to snack on an occasional mealworm. Gerbils love sunflower seeds and other fattening nuts. Feed your pets no more than a few nuts a week, because gerbils tend to get overweight. Gerbils do not drink much water, but you must still make sure your pets always have water available in their bottle.

GUINEA PIGS

Long and stout, with a belly that sweeps the ground, the guinea pig is a popular rodent that has been kept as a pet for centuries. Guinea pigs were first domesticated hundreds of years ago by South American Indians, who bred them from their tasty meat. In the sixteenth century, when European sailors returned from their conquests in South America, they also brought guinea pigs back to Europe.

In the wilds of South America, guinea pigs can be found living on the lower slopes of the Andes mountains. Groups of the guinea pigs live amongst rock outcrops and abandoned burrows dug by other animals. Just like North American marmots, the guinea pigs warn each other of danger by whistling and squealing.

Guinea pigs do not look very graceful. Tucked beneath their bellies are four short legs. They have large heads and appear to have no neck. Guinea pigs do not have a tail.

Many stories are told as to the origin of the name "guinea pig." Fanciers often prefer the more scientific name "cavy," and you might find guinea pigs sold as cavies in some pet stores.

WHICH KIND?

Guinea pigs come in a profusion of coat types, colors, and combinations of colors. Thirteen different breeds are recognized, all of which are similar in size. Guinea pigs of mixed breeds are commonly available.

Guinea pigs make lovable, low maintenance pets for children and adults alike. They rarely bite but it does take some time to tame them so they are not nervous being handled. Photo by Dr. Herbert R. Axelrod.

Guinea pigs are classified by coat type into three varieties. The smooth, short-haired, or American, guinea pigs have shiny, dense hair that feels sleek to touch. These are the easiest type to care for, because their coats do not need to be groomed. The rough-haired guinea pigs, or Abyssinians, have tuftlike rosettes of coarse hair all over the body and a ridge of hair along the back.

The long-haired guinea pigs, or Peruvians, have long silky hair that grows to the ground—and even longer if it is not kept trimmed. Because Peruvians' long hair falls over their faces, it can be difficult to tell their heads from their rear ends unless they are eating. They are often referred to by a variety of affectionate nicknames, such as dust mops. Peruvians attract a lot of attention, but before selecting this variety, be forewarned. Besides brushing their coat every few days, you will need to trim their hair and comb out the tangles each day.

Guinea pigs are available in a variety of colors including black, cream, chocolate, and gold and in many patterns such as Dutch (a white body with a pattern of one or two colors), Himalayan (a white body with colored points on the nose, feet, and ears), tortoise shell, and spotted (Dalmatian). The color or pattern you want might not always be available, but some pet stores can try to special order the variety you want.

When fully grown, a guinea pig is about seven to ten inches long and weighs between two and three pounds. The males are slightly larger than the females. Breeders call male guinea pigs boars and female guinea pigs sows.

MORE THAN ONE?

You can keep your pet guinea pig by itself if you have plenty of time to play with it. Otherwise, buy two young guinea pigs of the same sex and the same age. Ideally, you should buy your two guinea pigs at the same time. Two females will tend to get along better than two males.

THE RIGHT PET FOR YOU?

Guinea pigs are easy to care for and make gentle pets. Most guinea pigs are nervous and timid when you first bring them home. Some will squeal and run away when you put your hand into their cage.

With gentle handling, your pet will settle down quickly. Once tame, your guinea pig will sit calmly in your lap to be cuddled and petted, especially while eating a small piece of carrot. As with most other animals, abrupt movements and sudden noises will frighten your pet. Be careful when holding your guinea pig and protect it from falls or jumps. Because guinea pigs rarely, if ever bite, they make good pets for children.

Affectionate animals, guinea pigs become attached to their owners and look forward to regular playtime. The guinea pig is one of the

Dalmatian, golden, and lilac are but a few of the guinea pig coat colors. Photo by M. Gilroy.

few small animal pets that communicate vocally. Once your pet recognizes you, it will squeak and whistle excitedly when you come to play with it, especially if you have a food treat. Some guinea pigs whistle particularly loudly when they hear the refrigerator open! It can be fun to imitate your guinea pig's whistles and hear it answer you.

Guinea pigs make good classroom pets. Unlike other small furry animals, guinea pigs are active mainly in the daytime. Although placid and calm, guinea pigs sometimes suddenly jump up in the air and friskily bound in circles around their cage. Their sudden bursts of speed are amusing, as they joyously buck and race from one end of their cage to the other.

It is sometimes easier to describe a guinea pig by what it does not do rather than what it does. Low to the ground, guinea pigs are not agile or acrobatic. They do not climb or sit up. Instead of holding food in their paws, they eat with all four feet on the ground. Guinea pigs will not ride on a shoulder or in a pocket like a rat or a mouse. They cannot cling to and climb cage bars like a hamster. They cannot be trained to use a litter box when playing free in the house like a rabbit. Guinea pigs will not snuggle in a hammock like a ferret, nor will they run on an exercise wheel like hamsters and mice.

However, guinea pigs are good at eating. In between their naps, they will snack on their food throughout the day. They also drink a lot, between two and eight ounces (almost one cup) of water a day.

Guinea pigs, or cavies, come in a wide array of colors and coat types. Long-haired guinea pigs need regular brushing to keep a tidy coat. Photo by I. Francais.

This is a smooth tortoiseshell and white guinea pig. What a handsome fellow! Photo by Dr. Herbert R. Axelrod.

Guinea pigs especially appreciate some time outdoors in a safe pet play-pen. Photo by L. Van der Meid.

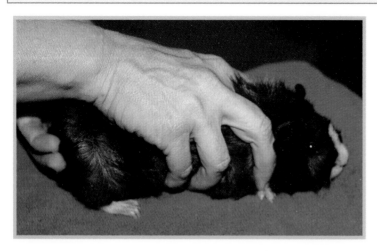

This is the proper method of holding an untamed guinea pig. Photo by L. Van der Meid.

A little guinea pig bath in the warm sunshine is a good idea provided the animal is well dried at the end. Photo by L. Van der Meid.

Long-coated cavies should be brushed every day to keep their coats from becoming tangled. Regular trims are required as well. Photo by L. Van der Meid.

Because they eat a lot, guinea pigs produce a lot of droppings, and they are one of the messiest small animals. Guinea pigs typically scatter their droppings throughout their cage. Unlike some other small pets, they are less likely to use one corner of their cage as a bathroom area. As a consequence, your pet's cage can become smelly and messy. This means that it can be more work to keep your guinea pig's cage clean compared to those of other types of small pets. You might have to totally or partially clean your pet's cage every few days.

Always use both hands to pick up your guinea pig. Slip one hand underneath your pet's belly, near its hind legs. Place your other hand over its shoulders so that it cannot squirm away and possibly fall. When you hold your pet, support its rear end with one hand and its front paws with your other hand. Then, for extra security, cradle your pet next to your body. Guinea pigs can be clumsy and are unafraid of heights. You must protect your pet from falling or jumping, which could seriously injure or even kill it.

A guinea pig's adult size can make it difficult for young children to hold. If a guinea pig feels insecure when held, it is more likely to struggle. Furthermore, even when trimmed, the feel of a guinea pig's nails frightens some young children, who might unintentionally drop their pet. Therefore it is best to have small children visit with their pet under parental supervision.

At least every few days, you should take your pet out of its cage to visit. If you have a back yard, you can make a portable grazing run constructed of wood and wire mesh for your guinea pig to use during warm weather. About one third of the run should be covered to protect your pet from the weather and to give it a place to retreat to if frightened.

Move the run from place to place so that your guinea pig has fresh (unfertilized) grass every day. Moving like a lawnmower, your pet will noisily grind its teeth as it eats. Unlike rabbits, guinea pigs do not dig.

Guinea pigs have a relatively long life span, between three and eight years. Keep this in mind when deciding whether you want such a pet.

SELECTING

Baby guinea pigs are precocial, which means they are born with fur and with their eyes open. They can run around right after birth. They begin to eat solid food by their second day, and they are weaned after three weeks. Baby guinea pigs are adorable and irresistible as they scamper around a cage. The best age at which a guinea pig should be bought is when it is six to eight weeks old.

Choose a lively guinea pig that does not cower and hide in a corner. One that is curious and interested in your hand, even if somewhat shy, will be a good pet. Short-haired guinea pigs are easier to care for than the long-haired breeds. The long-haired varieties need to be brushed each day and, because their hair grows continuously, it must be trimmed every few weeks. Guinea pigs with rosetted coats also need

In warm weather or climates, you can keep your guinea pigs in an outdoor hutch such as the one in this photo. Photo by G. Axelrod.

This is a young Peruvian guinea pig. Photo by M. Gilroy.

You will get great satisfaction from feeding your guinea pigs. They have good appetites. Photo by G. Axelrod.

regular grooming with a soft brush (e.g., a toothbrush).

HOUSING AND ACCESSORIES

Choose a roomy cage with a lot of floor space. Because guinea pigs do not climb they do not need tall cages. Two guinea pigs can be kept in a wire cage measuring at least 48 inches long by 24 inches wide by 20 inches high. Guinea pigs need cages with solid floors. Wire floors can make their feet sore, and their narrow feet can sometimes get caught and twisted in the wire. If you do use a wire cage, make sure the space between the floor wires is not greater than half an inch by half an inch. Place a layer of bedding over the wire bottom of the cage to make a protective, comfortable carpet for your guinea pig's feet.

A guinea pig can also be housed in a twenty-gallon glass aquarium. Although guinea pigs cannot jump, their aquarium should be covered with a wire screen to protect them from other animals. Aquariums do have a few drawbacks. They are heavy and can be difficult for children to clean. Because aquariums have less ventilation than a wire cage, they can become unhealthy for your pet if you do not change the bedding often enough.

Use shavings or a recycled paper product for bedding in your guinea pig's cage. Loose hay is good nesting material, and guinea pigs enjoy nibbling and burrowing through it. Provide a cozy nest box in which your guinea pig can sleep. Unlike other small furry pets, guinea pigs do not play with toys, but they will gnaw on chew products designed for use by them and some other small mammal pets.

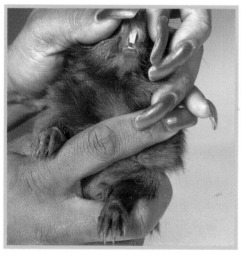

A guinea pig's teeth will grow continually. Be sure your pet has something to chew on to keep its teeth in proper trim. Photo by I. Francais.

Fresh water must be available at all times. Photo by L. Van der Meid.

FEEDING

Feed your pet a prepared diet of alfalfa pellets made specifically for guinea pigs. Like people, guinea pigs must derive vitamin C from their food, which is why it is important to feed them guinea pig food. The pellets made for rabbits look the same as guinea pig pellets, but they do not contain vitamin C. A guinea pig that is fed rabbit pellets will become sick and develop scurvy. Small pieces of fresh vegetable and fruit are good treats for your guinea pig.

Guinea pigs nibble throughout the day, so be sure your pet always has food. Feed your pet at the same time each day. Provide a gnawing block and a salt and mineral lick for them as well. Give your guinea pig fresh water in a water bottle.

Above: Young children love guinea pigs. They are large enough to cuddle and not so fast that they startle the child. Photo by I. Francais.

Right: A good cage should be easy to clean. With guinea pigs, the cage must be cleaned often. Photo by L. Van der Meid.

Be sure to dry your guinea pig well after its bath. Photo by L. Van der Meid.

This is a baby guinea pig. Don't hold your pet in an open hand unless you are sure it won't leap and injure itself. Photo by I. Francais.

GOLDEN HAMSTERS

The golden, or Syrian, hamster was originally captured for use in research. This rodent rose to world-wide prominence because it readily bred in captivity, whereas the Armenian and Chinese hamsters failed to breed in captivity. In 1931, a naturalist in Syria dug up a burrow containing a mother hamster and her litter for a researcher at Hebrew University in Jerusalem. Only three of the original group survived, one male and two females. It is believed that these three hamsters are the ancestors of most pet golden hamsters.

From the laboratories, the golden hamster found its way into the pet trade. The hamster's cute, roly-poly features and short tail help make it one of the most popular small animal pets in the world.

Hamsters are cute little animals with short legs and a small tail. They measure about six inches in length. Because they have poor vision, hamsters rely on their ears, nose, and whiskers to investigate their surroundings. Their keen sense of smell helps them find food and even helps them to recognize their owner. Secretions from skin glands located on their hips are used to mark their territory and attract a mate. Hamsters have large cheek pouches that extend down over their shoulders. They use their pouches to carry food back to their nest to store. In the wild, the habit of hoarding food helps hamsters survive when food is scarce.

WHICH KIND?

With more than thirty color varieties and three coat types, there is a hamster that will appeal to everyone. Some of the prettier colors are cream, fawn, and silver blue; hamsters also come in the pattern called piebald. You might find hamsters of three different kinds of coat at your pet store. The satin has a striking, shiny coat, the rex has short curly hair, and the long-haired looks just like the name.

In recent years, two species of dwarf hamsters have

This is the correct way to hold a hamster. Photo by I. Francais.

become commonly available as pets. The Siberian and Russian dwarf hamsters are smaller than the golden hamster, but their care is generally the same. Many of the original dwarf hamster stock came from Europe and Canada, where fanciers have been breeding them and developing unusual coat colors. Hamster fanciers have already started to develop new color mutations in these species, such as sapphire and pearl in the Siberian hamster. The work of developing new color and coat varieties of dwarf hamsters is just beginning and presents a challenging opportunity to interested and enthusiastic hamster owners.

Female hamsters are larger than male hamsters. The skin glands on the male hamster's hips are more obvious than those in the females. Some people think male hamsters are easier to tame than females, but it depends on the individual animal.

MORE THAN ONE?

A hamster must be kept by itself in its own cage. Your pet will not get lonely, because hamsters are not social animals. Unlike many other small furry pets, hamsters will fight if housed together. Chattering their teeth in anger and charging at each other, two fighting hamsters can be ferocious, even fighting until one is killed.

THE RIGHT PET FOR YOU?

Hamsters are one of the most popular small animal pets in the world, especially among children. Their popularity is probably because they are quiet, inexpensive,

This is a female golden hamster. Photo by M. Gilroy.

and easy to care for. With frequent handling and attention, your pet can become tame and will make a good pet.

Caring for a hamster and keeping it in a castle-like modular home is often a rite of childhood. The hamster's cute, roly-poly features appeal to children. Their small size makes them easy for children to hold. Because they readily breed, children can experience the pleasure of watching baby animals grow up.

Hamsters are low-maintenance pets. Most children can easily care for hamsters with minimal parental supervision, although parents of young children should know that the hamster's welfare will be partly their responsibility. Parents will need to oversee the hamster's care to make sure it is not neglected. Even when tame, hamsters do not need to be taken out to play every day as long as they have toys such as an exercise wheel in their cage. Because hamsters hoard food and do not drink large amounts of water, they can tolerate a *small* degree of occasional neglect. Even if they are not given as much attention as desirable, hamsters seldom become wild and easily frightened the way a neglected rabbit or guinea pig does. Your pet's cage will not need to be cleaned as frequently as other small animals, nor will its home become smelly very quickly.

You must be gentle and patient when taming your

Hamsters are nocturnal and are most active at night. During the day, your hamster will sleep curled up in a ball. One thing you must know about your hamster is that it does not like to be awakened when sleeping. Do not reach into your sleeping hamster's nest to take it out to play. Hamsters startled awake from their sleep can be grumpy, and many are likely to bite! Even a tame, friendly hamster might be nasty if disturbed while sleeping. Wait to play with your pet

and do not like their food-hoarding area disturbed.

Your pet will spend time fluffing its nest and investigating its cage. If your hamster is in a wire cage, it will climb along the top wires using only its two front paws.

To pick up your pet, slip one hand under its belly and quickly cup your other hand over its back and in front of its face. Always hold your hamster with both hands. Hamsters are wiggly and can suddenly jump out of your hands. Should your pet begin to squirm, bring it next to your body or return it to its cage. Do not hold it tighter! Some hamsters do not like to be held and are prone to biting if irritated.

Many hamsters must be held in cupped hands and continually "walked" between the hands. Before taking your pet home, ask a pet store employee to show you how to properly hold your pet. Knowing this will help you make friends faster with your pet and help reduce the risk of being nipped.

A hamster needs an exercise wheel. Running on a wheel will occupy your pet for hours. During the night, a hamster can travel up to five miles on its wheel. You can also let your hamster out of its cage to explore on the floor, but carefully watch your pet so that it does not escape. Hamsters have poor vision and are unafraid of heights. Your pet can easily fall off a table or bed and get hurt. One of the safest ways to play with your pet is in one of the roll-about balls or other toys made for hamsters.

Hamsters housed with toys are more active and interest-

Tame hamsters will eat right out of your hand. Photo by I. Francais.

hamster, as it can sometimes take several days or weeks to gain its trust. Offering a food treat is usually a good way to start making friends. Give your pet a few days to settle down before trying to hold it. Usually within a few days your pet will be more confident and might crawl onto your hand for a tidbit of food. Eventually you will be able to pick up and cuddle your hamster.

until it wakes up, usually in the late afternoon or early evening.

Hamsters are busy at night. Your pet will stuff food into its cheek pouches, scamper to a cage corner, and add the food to the store of food buried in the cage bedding. In between weekly cage cleanings, check on your pet's food hoard and remove any food that is spoiled. Be careful, though; some hamsters are territorial

ing to watch, and the animals are content and happier. They are playful animals that like to burrow and hide. Many toys have a practical function besides offering hamsters a form of entertainment. These include items such as wooden houses, which can be chewed to keep incisors trim. Toy shopping for a pet hamster is fun, since more colorful, appealing toys are made for hamsters than any other small animal. The opportunity to buy new toys for their pets to play with can help children maintain their interest.

Dwarf hamsters tend to be more active than the golden hamsters. They are also more easily awakened during the day, thus decreasing the likelihood that they will bite an unwary pet owner. Even more important is that when the dwarfs do bite, they rarely break the skin. Many dwarf hamsters are very curious and will run up to your hand to investigate.

Hamsters are one of the shorter-lived pocket pets. Expect to care for your hamster for about two years, sometimes three. The life span of dwarf hamsters is thought to be about that of golden hamsters.

CHOOSING YOUR HAMSTER

Choose a young hamster, about six to eight weeks old. Young hamsters are easier to tame than older ones. The best time to go hamster shopping is in the early evening or morning, because hamsters are most likely to be awake and active at those times. At other times of the day, hamsters will be sleeping in huge "hamster piles." Of course, the pet store employee

A light smoke pearl hamster. This dish of tasty hamster food could well end up in the hamster's cheek pouches to be hidden for later consumption. Photo by M. Gilroy.

Hamsters love toys and tunnels. Photo by I. Francais.

Keep track of how much food you give your hamster. If the leftovers are hidden and spoil, your hamster could get sick after eating it. Photo by I. Francais.

will wake them up for you. Aside from your preference for a certain color or coat type, a good choice is a hamster that sniffs your hand, lets you pet, or lets you hold it without struggling.

Be careful when choosing a pet dwarf hamster. Some strains are temperamental and ornery. Many breeders believe that hamsters are born with innate temperaments that cannot be changed by handling. Conscientious breeders select for docile, friendly animals. Aggressive hamsters with nasty dispositions are not bred and should not be sold as pets. Nonetheless, some dwarf hamsters might still tend to bite. As better dwarf hamster breeding continues, the hamsters should become less temperamental.

HOUSING AND ACCESSORIES

Your pet hamster can live in a wire cage, an aquarium with a cover, or a colorful modular cage made of hard plastic. Modular homes are flexible and encourage pet owners to customize their hamster's home by expanding it with tubes. Whatever type of cage you choose, it should measure at least 18 inches long by 12 inches wide by 10 inches high. Make sure it is sturdy and has a strong door latch. Because of their smaller feet, dwarf hamsters should be housed in cages with solid floors and sides. Place shavings on the bottom of your pet's cage. Provide commercial nesting material or hay for your hamster to use in building a nest.

Hamsters are one of the best, most persistent escape artists. They can squeeze out of the smallest opening. Your pet will exercise by climbing the bars of its cage looking for weak spots, and it can push and squeeze its way out of very small spaces. Some individual hamsters will try to chew out of their modular plastic homes, although most of those homes are now more secure because they come with chew-proof metal connectors that prevent hamsters from chewing out.

If your pet escapes, it could starve to death if not recaptured. Other pets, such as cats and dogs, might chase and kill your hamster. If you cannot find your pet, place the cage on the floor next to a wall. Leave the cage door open with a trail of shavings and food leading inside. Hopefully, your hamster will be in its cage the next morning.

Many toys have been designed for energetic hamsters. Your hamster will enjoy crawling through colorful plastic tubes, running on exercise wheels, and scampering up and down ladders. Give your hamster a place to sleep, such as a ceramic house or a wood house meant to be chewed. Use a plastic roll-about-ball to let your hamster safely explore a room.

FEEDING

Hamsters are easy to feed. A variety of nutritionally complete, prepared hamster mixes are available from your local pet store. Always be sure your pet has food in his dish. However, your hamster will store the tastier tidbits of food in a cage corner under the bedding. Feed him small pieces of fresh vegetables and fruits as treats, but give him only as much as he can eat in a few minutes and remove any excess. Fresh foods that are stored in your hamster's hoard could spoil and cause him to become ill. Provide fresh water in a water bottle.

This is a female cinnamon Russian dwarf hamster, taking life easy. Photo by M. Gilroy.

RABBITS

Almost everyone can recognize a rabbit with its long hind legs, short fluffy tail, and long ears. A rabbit's large eyes are placed on the sides of its head. This position helps a rabbit see behind it almost as well as it can see in front. Like guinea pigs, rabbits do not hold food in their front paws, but eat with all four feet on the ground.

Because they have six incisor teeth, rabbits are classified as lagomorphs, not rodents. Animals classified as rodents have only four incisor teeth. Although hard to see on your pet, rabbits have two tiny teeth located behind their upper incisors.

People began breeding the specialized varieties of rabbits found today more than one hundred years ago. Domesticated rabbits have been introduced by people, accidentally and intentionally, to most parts of the world.

Yes, it's a live rabbit, not a stuffed toy. This is the breed known as English Angora. Photo by I. Francais.

This is a lop-eared rabbit. The length of the ears on some lops is as much as 30 inches! Photo by B. Crook.

WHICH KIND?

Rabbits come in a wide range of colors and sizes and a variety of coat types. At least forty breeds of pedigreed rabbits are recognized.

The smallest breed, the Netherland dwarf, weighs only about two pounds and is a popular pet. The largest breed, the Flemish giant, weighs more than fourteen pounds. Although they make friendly pets, rabbits are used mainly for meat and fur. Just like the different breeds of dogs and cats have their fans, so do the different rabbit breeds.

Some rabbit breeds, such as the Flemish giant, are hard to find. Others, such as the various kinds of lop-eared rabbits, are more commonly available.

When choosing your pet rabbit, remember that some of the larger breeds can weigh more than ten pounds and be difficult to handle, even for an adult. Large breeds also need large cages. The long-haired Angora looks like an adorable, animated stuffed animal. But this breed is not a good choice for a first-time owner, because you must groom an Angora every day. Some rabbits are mixed breeds and, just as with dogs, you will not know

for sure how large they will grow.

Female rabbits are called does and male rabbits are called bucks. The does are slightly larger than the bucks. Male rabbits that are unneutered often spray urine near their cage and when let out to play.

MORE THAN ONE?

A solitary rabbit will make a good pet as long as you have enough time to give it attention each day. Rabbits are social animals. If you will not be able to give your rabbit daily playtime, buy two young rabbits. You can keep two females together. A male and

female can be kept together, but they will have babies unless at least one of them is neutered. Two males can be kept together only if they are neutered, otherwise they will fight.

A veterinarian can spay or neuter your rabbit. This procedure will prevent unwanted baby rabbits. Some rabbit experts recommend neutering your rabbit because doing so can reduce aggression and territorial marking (for example, spraying urine) and will make your pet calmer. If you buy two rabbits, be aware that in a pair one rabbit will attempt to dominate the other, and they may fight.

This fellow enjoys the "run of the house." Rabbits need not be kept locked away. They are clean animals that can be litter-box trained. Photo by B. Crook.

RABBITS

THE RIGHT PET FOR YOU?

Pet rabbits are hardy and easy to care for. A rabbit that is well socialized to people will be affectionate and friendly. Rabbits are responsive pets and can learn their names. Some rabbits even learn commands such as "come" and "no." Tame rabbits enjoy interacting with their owners. When your pet wants to play, it might bump into your leg and dash away. You will see your pet stand up on its hind legs and sniff when it wants to learn more about its surroundings.

While some rabbits enjoy being petted and held, many rabbits prefer a scratch behind their ears. Your rabbit might willingly sit on your lap for a few moments, but it will usually prefer to be on the ground exploring. It will take a few weeks for you to tame your rabbit. The more time you spend playing with it, the sooner you will have a tame and friendly pet. Rabbits are

English Angora rabbits are often kept for their fur, which is spun into wool for clothing. Photo by I. Francais.

most active in the early morning and evening.

Rabbits are a good alternative for people who live in apartments and cannot own a cat or a dog. A pet rabbit does not need as much attention as a dog or even a ferret, and it will still bond with you and make a wonderful pet. However, if you neglect your rabbit and do not give it enough attention, your pet can become skittish and easily frightened.

You might then find it difficult to hold your rabbit without having it kick and scratch. Choose a rabbit only if you can devote some time to playing with it each day. Also consider that rabbits have a fairly long life span, between six and ten years.

A rabbit should be let out of its cage several times each week. It will be obvious that your pet enjoys its exercise time as it hops and runs around, occasionally leaping in the air. Be sure to watch your pet when it is out of its cage. Rabbits have a habit of chewing and grinding their teeth on almost everything. Clapping your hands and shouting "no!" will cause your pet to stop what it is doing.

Indoor rabbits need to have their toenails trimmed when they get too long. This is the proper way to hold the animal while trimming its nails. Photo by L. Van der Meid.

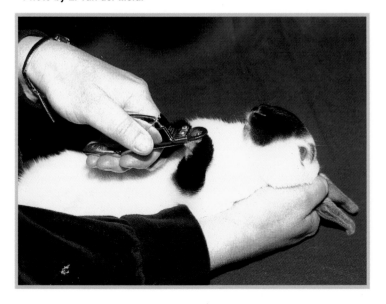

Your pet could accidentally escape outside if people are coming in and out of your house while your pet is loose. It is safest to limit your rabbit's explorations to one room with the door closed.

You can build your rabbit a grazing run similar to the one described in the section about guinea pigs. However, because rabbits dig, the bottom of the run must have a wire floor. Your pet can then safely graze outside in its run. Some rabbits can be trained to walk on a harness and lead, but they will not walk on a lead like an obedient dog. If you train your pet to get used to a leash and harness inside, you can then take your rabbit outside and let it graze and sunbathe. Be careful of other animals and sudden movements, which might frighten your rabbit and cause it to bolt.

Because they are large animals, rabbits produce a lot of urine and droppings. Many rabbits will use one corner of

their cage for a toilet area. Cleaning this area each day will help reduce any odor. If your pet's home is large enough, place a small animal litter pan in the cage, away from your pet's food bowl. Just like ferrets, many rabbits can be trained to use a litter box both in their cages and when they are outside their cages.

Because of rabbits' relatively large size, use two hands to pick up and hold your pet. Use one hand to lift and support the animal's rear end and your other hand to grab the loose skin at the base of its neck. Hold your rabbit in your arms next to your body for extra security. As long as you are gentle, your pet will not mind being picked up and held for short periods of time. Be careful with large rabbits. They can kick and scratch if they do not want to be held. Your pet could get injured if you drop it.

Rabbits are clean animals and constantly groom them-

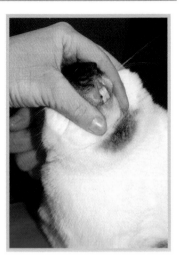

Nylabone Edible Carrot Chew Sticks for Rabbits will keep your rabbit's teeth from becoming overgrown and out of align. Overgrown teeth often have to be filed down at the vet's office. Photo by L. Van der Meid

selves. Like cats, rabbits can get furballs and become constipated. They also molt several times a year and can shed on your clothes. Brushing your pet can help prevent furballs and will help reduce shedding. You will probably need to occasionally trim your rabbit's nails. Two people are often required, one to hold the rabbit and the other to trim the nails. If necessary, your veterinarian can trim your pet's claws.

It is highly unusual for "pocket" pets to have fleas. However, fleas can be transmitted to your rabbit from other household pets, such as a dog or cat. You can use a flea comb to remove any fleas from your rabbit. Cat flea products are usually safe to use on rabbits, but check with your veterinarian to be sure.

CHOOSING YOUR RABBIT
Choose a rabbit that's young but not too young; one

This is a smoke pearl mini rex rabbit, a handsome breed with a very plush coat. Photo by I. Francais.

at least eight weeks old would be good. The size of a young rabbit will vary, depending on the breed. The rabbit's coat should look glossy and the rabbit should look solid, without any bones showing.

Ideally, the rabbit you want will sniff your hand and not hide in a corner of the cage. When properly held, the rabbit should relax, not struggle and scratch.

Different breeds of rabbits were developed for different purposes, such as for meat or fur, and each breed varies in personality and temperament.

Your rabbit's coat should be brushed or combed often to decrease shedding. Photo by I. Francais.

Do some research and talk to people who know about rabbits to help you select a rabbit that is right for you.

HOUSING AND ACCESSORIES

While rabbits make good apartment pets, they do need roomy cages. Even the small breeds should be housed in large cages. While the actual cage size depends on the adult size of your rabbit, expect to buy a cage that measures around three feet long . Larger breeds, such as French lops, will need a larger cage. In general, the bigger the cage the better, although finding a place to keep a large cage in your house can sometimes be a problem. Because rabbits like to stand up on their hind feet, their cage should be tall enough that they can do so.

The cage should provide plenty of floor space, with enough room for a sleeping box.

Shavings and a layer of hay for nibbling make good bedding for your rabbit. If the cage is large enough, a small animal litter pan can be left in it for your rabbit to use. Also place shavings in the litter pan.

Rabbits are susceptible to foot problems if they are not housed properly. Rabbits are usually housed on a wire floor so that their droppings and urine fall through to the tray below. If the floor spacing is too large (which can vary depending on the breed of rabbit), the wire might be uncomfortable for a rabbit and its feet can fall through the spaces. Some individuals develop sore hocks if housed

directly on wire. Providing a solid floor by either piling shavings up over the wire or by giving the rabbit a piece of plywood on which to rest can help solve this problem.

FEEDING

Feed your rabbit alfalfa pellets made for rabbits, along with loose hay and alfalfa blocks. In addition, your pet will enjoy treats of fresh cabbage, carrots, dandelions, and clover. Pet stores sell some food treats that your rabbit will relish. Gradually add fresh greens to your rabbit's diet, but give only as much as your pet will eat in a half hour. Because rabbits eat throughout the day, they should always have food available. Rabbits drink a lot of water, so be sure their water bottle is always full.

FANCY MICE

Fancy mice are a domesticated form of the house mouse. The house mouse is a rodent that has been selectively bred in captivity for more than a century. It was first domesticated as a small laboratory animal for use in scientific research. Fancy mice have been kept as pets almost as long as they have been used in laboratories. The National Mouse Club of Great Britain, for example, was formed in 1895!

WHICH KIND?

Decades of selective breeding have produced more than fifty color varieties of mice, and four coat types have been developed: satin, astrex, long-haired, and rex. Marked varieties include broken-marked mice, which have colored spots or patches distributed over a white background.

When fully grown, mice measure between four to six

This is a female black Dutch mouse. Photo by M. Gilroy

inches in body length. They have a slender pink tail that is almost as long as their body. Their tails are prehensile and help them to climb. Male mice are called bucks and females are called does. Males use urine to mark their territory and have a very strong "mousy" smell.

MORE THAN ONE?

You can keep one mouse by itself, but mice live most happily in pairs, such as two females or a male and a female (if you want baby mice). Because they fight when grown, do not keep male mice together. It can be difficult to add a new mouse to an existing cage of mice. The new mouse will often be attacked. Introduce the new mouse by keeping it in a separate cage placed next to the other mice cage for about one week before trying to add the new mouse.

THE RIGHT PET FOR YOU?

If you want a pet that is interesting and easy to care for, the mouse might be the right pet for you. Although they do not have the allure of some of the larger pets, mice make good pets, since they do not require any specialized care. Because of their tiny

This neat little pet carrier is a perfect mouse house. Photo by I. Francais.

This is a lilac and white mouse. Photo by M. Gilroy.

Upper right: This agouti female mouse is investigating the tennis ball in the hopes of having a new home. Photo by M. Gilroy.

These are bat-eared mice. The lighter colored mouse is called a "lilac." Photo by M. Gilroy.

An albino mouse investigates a new exercise wheel. Photo by M. Gilroy.

size, mice are especially appealing to children, who can easily hold and play with their pets. Very young children should be supervised while playing with a mouse, since they might accidentally squeeze their pet and seriously hurt it. Pet mice live about two years.

Mice can be timid, but if you treat your pets with kindness, they will respond well and become friendly. Some mice seem to enjoy crawling on their owners and

Although you might be able to pick your mouse up in one hand, be sure to use two hands to hold your pet. Some mice are wiggly and will not hold still. You might have to "walk" it between your two hands. To prevent your mouse from jumping out of your hands, place one hand in front of your mouse's head. If necessary, you can gently hold your pet near the base of its tail for added security. Never tightly hold your mouse to prevent it from getting

time during both the day and night. If their cage is full of interesting toys, mice are entertaining to watch. They dash about their cage, darting into cardboard tubes, dangling from a ladder, and frolicking with one another. Mice like toys, and it is fun to provide them with new and interesting ones. Put some unscented tissue or cardboard tubes in your pets' cage at night. The next morning you might find that your pets have shredded the items and

Domestic mice are available in a variety of colors. Photo by M. Gilroy.

playing hide-n-seek in shirt pockets and collars. If you use a tasty treat, such as a tidbit of cracker, your mouse will quickly become your friend. Young mice become tame sooner than older ones. Give your pet the chance to know you without feeling threatened, by placing your hand inside its cage. Your pet might smell and walk on your hand, but it should not nip you. If your mouse seems afraid, place your hand with a food treat into its cage before trying to pick it up.

away. Instead, cup your pet against your body. Although mice bite infrequently, they will bite if they are scared. If your pet seems frightened, return it to its home for a while.

Mice like to be let out of their cages to play and explore. Because of their small size it is best to limit their play area to the top of a bed or a couch. Watch your pets carefully. They can quickly disappear!

Like gerbils, mice are awake for short periods of

added them to their nest. Mice enjoy climbing up and down a thick parrot rope dangling from the roof of their cage, tunneling through cardboard tubes, and running on their exercise wheel.

Unfortunately, mice can be smelly. Your pet's cage needs to be cleaned frequently to prevent odor. How often will depend on how many mice you have. The more mice you have in a cage the more often you will have to clean the cage. For example, a group of mice might need their cage cleaned at least twice a week. If you have male mice, you may want to clean their cage as often as every other day. Unfortunately, few mice establish a bathroom area in a corner of their cage. Most mice defecate anywhere, even in their food dish. This is one reason why you might need to clean their cage more often. Using bedding with odor control properties will help reduce any smell.

SELECTING

Many of the mice sold in pet stores end up as food for reptiles such as snakes and large lizards. Because these mice will be food, they are not always healthy. Tell the pet store employees that you want a mouse for a pet so they can show you the best mice the store carries.

Try to choose a mouse that is calm when held. Do not buy a mouse that nips. A baby mouse can be bought when it is about four weeks old. Young mice become tame more quickly than older ones, and they make better pets. Check to be sure the mouse you want has no lumps, bumps, or scabs.

HOUSING AND ACCESSORIES

Mice do best in roomy cages that allow them space to climb, jump, and run. A mouse cage should measure at least 15 inches long by 10 inches wide by 10 inches high. Mice can be housed in wire cages as long as the space between the wires is not larger than one quarter of an inch. Mice can squeeze out of larger spaces. A ten-gallon aquarium is large enough for a small group of mice. Be sure to cover the aquarium with a

A male bat-eared mouse. Photo by M. Gilroy.

wire screen that clips securely to the cage. Mice can jump out of an uncovered aquarium. Mice are curious animals and will escape if they can find a way out of their cage.

Because mice do not burrow, use a shallow layer of shavings in their cage. Give your mice a nest box in which to sleep. They will make a comfortable nest out of unscented tissue paper, commercial nesting material, or an old sock. Provide your mice with toys. Besides toys made for mice, those designed for hamsters and wooden toys sold for birds can also be used. An exercise wheel, paper towel tubes, ladders, swings, and nuts in a shell will give your pet hours of entertainment. Some of your

mouse's toys will pick up a "mousy" smell and will need to be replaced.

FEEDING

Mice are omnivorous and eat a variety of fruits and vegetables, grains, seeds, nuts, and meat. A hamster or gerbil mix is a good basic diet for your mice. Also add different types of bird seed to the mix, such as parakeet, finch, and parrot food. Mice eat throughout the day and night and should always have food available. Feed your mouse only small amounts of fresh foods, such as carrots and apples. Mice also enjoy treats such as honey seed sticks, hard dog biscuits, and an occasional small mealworm. Give them fresh water in a water bottle.

FANCY RATS

Rats are rodents that are found all over the world; there are many different species. The two most infamous species are the destructive brown and black rats, which have lived with people for centuries. The fancy rats sold in pet stores are descendants of the brown rat. It is thought that the brown rat was first domesticated for use in ratting contests with dogs. Around the turn of the last century, rats were being used for scientific studies. From the laboratory, rats found their way into homes as pets.

The first thing most people notice about rats is their long scaly tail. "Yuck," they say. But a rat's tail serves several useful functions, and the charms of a pet rat outweigh any beauty flaws. Their tails help them

Rats are intelligent and affectionate pets with clean habits. Photo by I. Francais.

A young Siamese male rat and a young chocolate female rat. Photo by M. Gilroy.

balance when climbing, and the scales can ruffle backward and give them a good grip. Rats lack sweat glands, but they can use their tails as thermoregulating devices. When a rat is cold, the blood vessels in its tail constrict and conserve heat. When a rat is hot, the same vessels radiate excess heat.

WHICH KIND?

Pet rats come in a variety of fancy colors and markings. Black, champagne, albino, creme, lilac, and agouti are some of the most common colors. The most common marked variety is the hooded rat, which has a colored hood that covers its head and shoulders and continues down the rat's back. Rats come in three different coat types:

smooth, curly-coated rex, and hairless. A tailless rat has been developed, but it is not yet commonly available.

When fully grown a rat measures about twenty inches in length, including its long, scaly tail. Female rats are called does and male rats are called bucks. Female rats are smaller than male rats. Both sexes make excellent pets, but like many other male mammals, male rats are more likely to mark their territory with urine.

MORE THAN ONE?

Rats are social animals and enjoy each other's company. However, it is not necessary to keep rats together as long as you give your pet plenty of attention. Rats of either sex can be kept together, if purchased at the same time. Usually one rat will be dominant over the other.

This is the correct way to hold a rat. Be sure you gain the animal's trust before you attempt to restrain it. Photo by I. Francais.

This is a black hooded rat. Rats make great use of exercise wheels. Photo by M. Gilroy.

THE RIGHT PET FOR YOU?

Many people dislike rats because of their long scaly tails. But if you can forget your dislike of a rat's tail and the bad reputation of their wild relatives, you would find that rats make one of the best small animal pets. They are friendly, affectionate, and curious. Rats thrive on human companionship and look forward to interacting with their owner. Most rats stand at their cage door in the evening asking to come out and play.

Rats are playful and enjoy chasing and tackling a piece of paper tied to a string. Pay attention when your pet is exploring outside its cage. Your pet might chew on items, and some rats will cart off papers and other objects to take to their secret hiding places. Rats have good memories and are extremely intelligent. Many scientists believe that rats are among the smartest animals. Your rat will learn its name and can be trained to come to you when called. Many pet rat owners train their rats to perform neat tricks such as walking on their hind legs and how to run through a maze to reach a food reward.

Rats are nocturnal and are most active in the evening. Unlike small animals such as hamsters, most rats will not use an exercise wheel. They prefer to be taken out of their cage to play with you and explore a room. Rats are naturally clean animals and groom themselves throughout the day.

It is fun to let your rat ride on your shoulder, in a shirt sleeve, or tucked in a large shirt pocket. Rats are easy to care for and fun to feed. Besides their regular diet, it is fun to share a small piece of a sandwich with your pet. Rats can be let out of their cage to play and explore. However, they do tend to mark their trail with urine.

Tame rats are docile and will not struggle or jump out of your hands. To pick up your pet, scoop your hand underneath its belly and let it rest in both hands. Hold your pet next to your body for extra protection.

Rat owners can become very attached to their pets. However, rats live for only about three years.

CHOOSING YOUR RAT

Choose a young rat four to eight weeks old. Try to choose a curious rat. When you put your hand into the pet store's cage, many of the rats might scurry away. But some will quickly return to inspect your hand. Some rats relax right away when you hold them and will make good pets. Other rats might be frightened and tense. If the rat you want does not calm down after being held awhile, it is best to choose another one. Avoid selecting a rat that sniffles when it breathes, as this usually indicates an incurable chronic respiratory infection.

HOUSING AND ACCESSORIES

House your rat in a wire small mammal cage, wire bird cage, or ten-gallon aquarium covered with a screen that fastens with secure clips. The cage should measure at least 20 inches long by 10 inches wide by 12 inches high. Use a larger cage for a pair of rats. If you use a wire cage, make sure the space between the bars is no larger than one half of an inch or your rat might be able to squeeze out of the cage. Pine shavings and recycled paper products are good choices for bedding.

Rats need a nesting box for sleeping. You can buy one at a pet store or make one from an empty box. Place the box high in the cage, as rats like to climb and perch. Give them an old sock for nesting material. Your rat will play on wooden toys, such as ladders and swings.

FEEDING

Rats are omnivorous and eat fruits, vegetables, grains, seeds, nuts, and meat. Provide your rat with a nutritious diet by giving it a hamster or gerbil mix. You can add some types of bird seed, such as wildbird seed, dry unsweetened cereals, bread, and crackers to this mix. Hard dog biscuits are also good for your rat and will help keep its teeth trim. You can also give your pet nutritionally balanced laboratory pellets made especially for rats.

Rats enjoy treats of fruits, vegetables, and table scraps, such as baked potato skin. Remember to remove any uneaten moist foods and to feed only as much as your rat will eat in one sitting. Your rat should always have food available. Provide fresh water in a water bottle.

Rats are playful and inquisitive. You don't have to buy special toys, but do make sure the toys you offer them can't be chewed. Photo by M. Gilroy.

HEDGEHOGS

Hedgehogs are found in Europe, Africa, and Asia. They live in a variety of habitats including deciduous forests, scrub, rocky enclaves, grasslands, and deserts. In the wild, most hedgehogs hibernate during the cold winter months. Desert-dwelling species sometimes estivate for a few weeks during the hot summer. Hedgehogs are covered with spines, which are modified hairs that taper to a very sharp point. Hedgehogs are nocturnal and primarily carnivorous; they prey on insects, invertebrates, and even lizards and baby mice. Hedgehogs usually have thirty-six teeth, most of which are sharp and pointed.

WHICH KIND?

The African pygmy hedgehog, which is native to many parts of Africa and southern Europe, is the species most commonly offered for sale.

When fully grown, it will measure about seven inches long and weigh a little more than one pound. It is usually colored a mixture of brown, black, and white. Some individuals are lighter and some are darker, but breeders have not yet developed many color mutations, although albino, cream, snowflake (all white with a dark mask and dark eye color), and polka dot (a striped or mottled appearance) hedgehogs are sometimes available.

Male hedgehogs are called boars and females are called sows. Females are often larger than the males.

White African pygmy hedgehog. Hedgehogs are primarily insectivores, and while they do well on prepared foods, appreciate mealworms and other live foods from time to time. Photo by I. Francais.

Hedgehogs are primarily nocturnal animals that mostly sleep during the day. Photo by R. Lermayer.

A properly equipped hedgehog home includes a place where your "hog" can sleep in peace. Photo by R. Lermayer.

MORE THAN ONE?

Hedgehogs are solitary animals and should be housed by themselves.

THE RIGHT PET FOR YOU?

Hedgehogs appeal to people who are looking for an unusual animal. They are quiet, friendly, curious pets, but some can be timid and nervous. Compared to other small pets, hedgehogs are expensive. Hedgehogs are relatively odorless. They live between four and six years.

Hedgehogs are cute-looking, but if you want a soft cuddly animal, the hedgehog is not for you. Their spines are sharp and can hurt. Because of their spines, hedgehogs are not good pets for young children. The hedgehog is not spiny on its face, chest, throat, belly, and legs. Young hedgehogs have sharper spines than do older animals. Just as other pets lose hair, hedgehogs molt a few spines at a time.

Handle your pet every day so that it stays tame. Hedgehogs that are regularly handled from a young age develop into friendly pets. Pick up your hedgehog by scooping your hand underneath its belly. Use both hands to cradle your pet close to your body. Once a hedgehog is used to being held, it will leave its spines flat. Tame hedgehogs let you scratch their chin and belly. You can pet your hedgehog when its spines are flat against its body. Some hedgehogs lick and then nip fingers. You can say "no" to discourage this behavior, but do not hit your pet. Once your hedgehog knows you, this behavior will stop.

You must handle your pet every day so that it stays tame and friendly. Since hedgehogs are nocturnal, early evening is the best time to play with them. When you let your hedgehog out of its cage, your pet will waddle around the room as it explores. It will not be destructive, but you should still supervise your pet when it is loose.

Hedgehogs have an interesting behavior called "self-anointing." When a hedgehog smells a certain odor, such as perfume, it produces a foamy saliva that it coats its body with. Experts are uncertain what this behavior means, but it usually stops once the hedgehog is familiar with the scent. You will not need to brush your pet. However,

If this dog takes any further liberties, it will soon have a very sore nose. Hedgehogs roll into a tight ball and then give a little *bounce* that gives its sharp quills extra pricking power. Photo by R. Lermayer.

hedgehogs need to have their toenails clipped regularly. Use a pair of human or cat nail clippers to clip your pet's nails.

Like ferrets, hedgehogs are not legal to keep as pets in all states (e.g., they are prohibited in California). Generally if they are offered for sale in a pet store, they are legal to own in that store's state. But of course laws can change from time to time. What is illegal today might be legal tomorrow—and vice versa.

CHOOSING YOUR HEDGE-HOG

It is best to choose a young hedgehog that is already hand tamed. Older hedgehogs that have not been handled do not make good pets.

A tame hedgehog will lay its spines flat and not roll into a prickly ball. Avoid choosing a nervous hedgehog that curls into a ball (especially if it stays in a tight ball) and clicks, hisses, or attempts to bite.

A healthy hedgehog's nose should be dry to slightly moist, without signs of discharge or swelling. Check that the fur on the hedgehog's belly is clean and dry.

HOUSING AND ACCESSORIES

A hedgehog should be kept in a large roomy cage, one that measures at least 48 inches long by 36 inches wide by 18 inches high. Aquariums with screen covers (since hedgehogs can climb), indoor rabbit hutches, or plastic dog or cat carrying cages are all housing options. Some

African pygmy hedgehogs are not particularly busy, but they do appreciate exploring new objects in their homes. Photo by I. Francais.

Get to know your hedgehog before you try to handle it. They are really quite easy to tame as long as you don't frighten them. Photo by I. Francais.

Here is a little girl who has earned the trust of her friendly hedgehog. Hedgehogs will not prick unless they feel threatened. Photo by I. Francais

It's fine to take your hedgehog outdoors in good weather; just make sure it doesn't get lost! Photo by R. Lermayer.

hedgehogs like the two-story cages sold for guinea pigs. In a wire cage, the shavings should cover the floor to prevent your pet's feet from getting caught and twisted in the wire.

Provide your pet with a nest box or a hollow plastic tube for a bedroom. Place a small animal litter pan in a corner of your hedgehog's cage, away from its feeding and sleeping areas. Your hedgehog will use the pan as a toilet.

Hedgehogs will use exercise wheels. They need a solid-floor wheel or a wire wheel with one-eighth of an inch mesh, because their feet can get caught and twisted in the standard wire exercise wheels.

FEEDING

Pet hedgehogs are fairly easy to feed. Your hedgehog's basic diet should be a commercial dry food formulated specifically for hedgehogs. If this is unavailable, feed a high-quality "lite" dry cat food sold only at pet shops. Supplement your pet's diet with treats of cottage cheese, hard-boiled egg, pieces of meat, and mealworms. Hedgehogs enjoy treats of small pieces of fruit or vegetables.

Adjust the amount of food you feed your hedgehog by watching how much he eats. Hedgehogs do best with small meals, rather than one large meal. Hedgehogs have a tendency to become obese. You will need to monitor how much food you feed your pet to prevent it from becoming overweight. (In the wild, hedgehogs must gain weight to survive their winter hibernation or summer estivation.)

Give your hedgehog fresh water in a water bottle.